The Mummy Stays in Egypt!

History Stories for Children
Children's Ancient History

BABY PROFESSOR
EDUCATION KIDS

In this book, we're going to talk about mummies in Egypt. So, let's get right to it!

WHY DID THE EGYPTIANS MUMMIFY DEAD BODIES?

The Ancient Egyptians worshipped many different gods. They believed that when someone passed away they would be alive again in the "afterlife." They also believed that the person's life in the afterlife would be very similar to the life he or she had already lived on Earth.

EGYPTIAN MUMMY

Egyptians were buried with all their important personal possessions and it was vital that their bodies be preserved so they could travel on their next journey. Eventually, the dead person would reclaim his or her body so the body had to be recognizable. The Egyptians were successful in doing this, because the facial features of unwrapped mummies can still be seen today even though they are thousands of years old.

THE MYTH OF OSIRIS

There is an Egyptian myth that tells the story of the very first mummy.

Osiris and his wife, who was named Isis, ruled Egypt. They loved each other and through their magic they built Egypt into a rich, peaceful civilization. However, all was not as it seemed. Osiris had a brother by the name of Seth. Seth wanted to be the powerful Pharaoh, ruler of Egypt, but his brother Osiris was standing in his way. He created a plan to get rid of Osiris.

Osiris

He built an elaborate chest that was designed to fit his brother's body. He said he would give this amazing chest to anyone who could fit inside. Many people tried to climb in, but they couldn't fit because the chest was

designed for Osiris. When Osiris got into the chest, it fit him perfectly. Seth quickly sealed the chest and threw it into the Nile River. Now his brother would be out of the way and he could be Pharaoh.

Isis

I sis was grief stricken when she couldn't find Osiris. She went in search of him and traveled everywhere. When Seth found out that Isis was looking for Osiris, he went to find the chest and destroy the evidence of what he had done. He found it and opened it. He cut his brother's body into pieces and scattered them far away from each other.

Isis discovered what had happened. She found all of Osiris's pieces and put him back together. She wrapped his body pieces with linen cloth cut into strips like bandages. Osiris was the first mummy. When Isis was finished, she used her powers to give him life again. Osiris told his beloved wife that he had to leave to go into the afterlife. He became the god of the underworld.

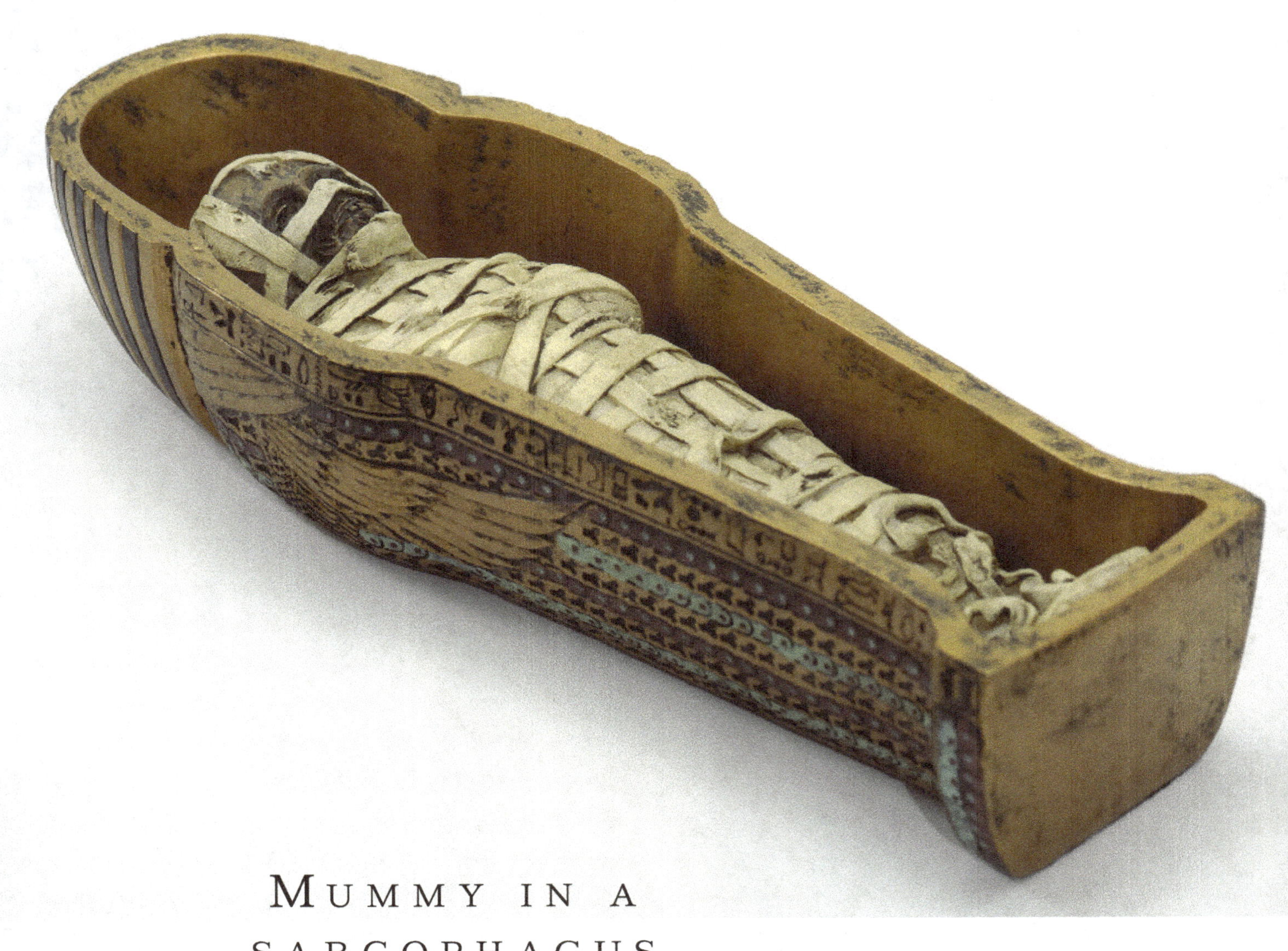

Mummy in a
sarcophagus

WHEN DID THE EGYPTIANS BEGIN TO MUMMIFY BODIES?

Around 3500 BC, the Egyptians began to use a very complicated process to mummify dead bodies. The process they used was a type of embalming to prevent the body from decay.

Mummification was expensive, so only the Pharaohs and wealthy received the most advanced mummification processes. Others were mummified using a process

with fewer steps so it would be less expensive. The Egyptians also mummified animals of all types. Cats were admired, so thousands of cats were mummified.

WHAT WERE THE STEPS USED TO MAKE A MUMMY?

Those dead bodies that received the best mummification went through a process that took about 70 days. Those who received the inexpensive embalming were completed within a week.

The embalmer was a masterful temple priest who understood the physical body as well as the religious and spiritual meaning of the process. He wore a mask of the god Anubis, who had the head of a jackal and the body of a man.

MUMMY

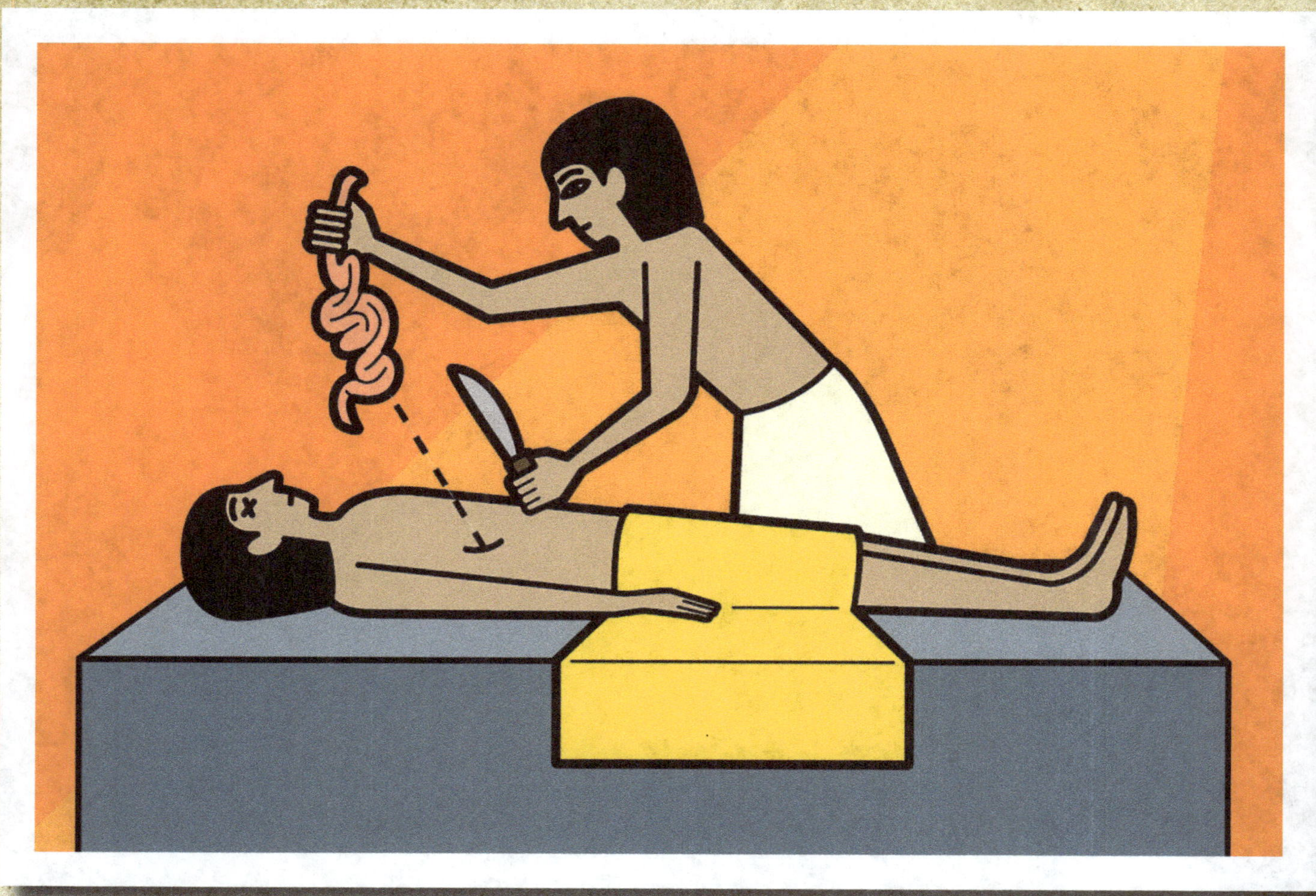

FIRST STEP IN
EMBALMING

The first step was to remove the moister parts of the body that could rot. The brain tissue was carefully removed through the nostrils and thrown away. This had to be done in a way that wouldn't hurt the facial features, because the person had to be able to recognize himself.

The next step was to make an incision on the body's left side. Both lungs as well as the liver and stomach were mummified separately, and placed into special containers that were canopic jars. The intestines were mummified separately too.

The Egyptians didn't think the brain was important to preserve, but they did believe the heart was vital.

The heart was left inside the body, because the person's heart would determine if he or she would be allowed to proceed to the afterlife.

Anubis

The heart was judged by the actual god Anubis when the person died. If the heart was good, it was as light as the "Feather of Truth and Justice." A person who had a light heart would be able to enter the afterlife. If the person was evil, then his or her heart was heavy and it would be eaten by the demon Ammit. She was part crocodile, part lion, and part hippo.

O nce the organs were removed, the body was covered with a salt-like substance called natron. This part of the process took about 40 days and dissolved the body's fats as well as absorbed its moisture.

Linen cloth was used inside the cavities and the body was preserved using oils and herbs.

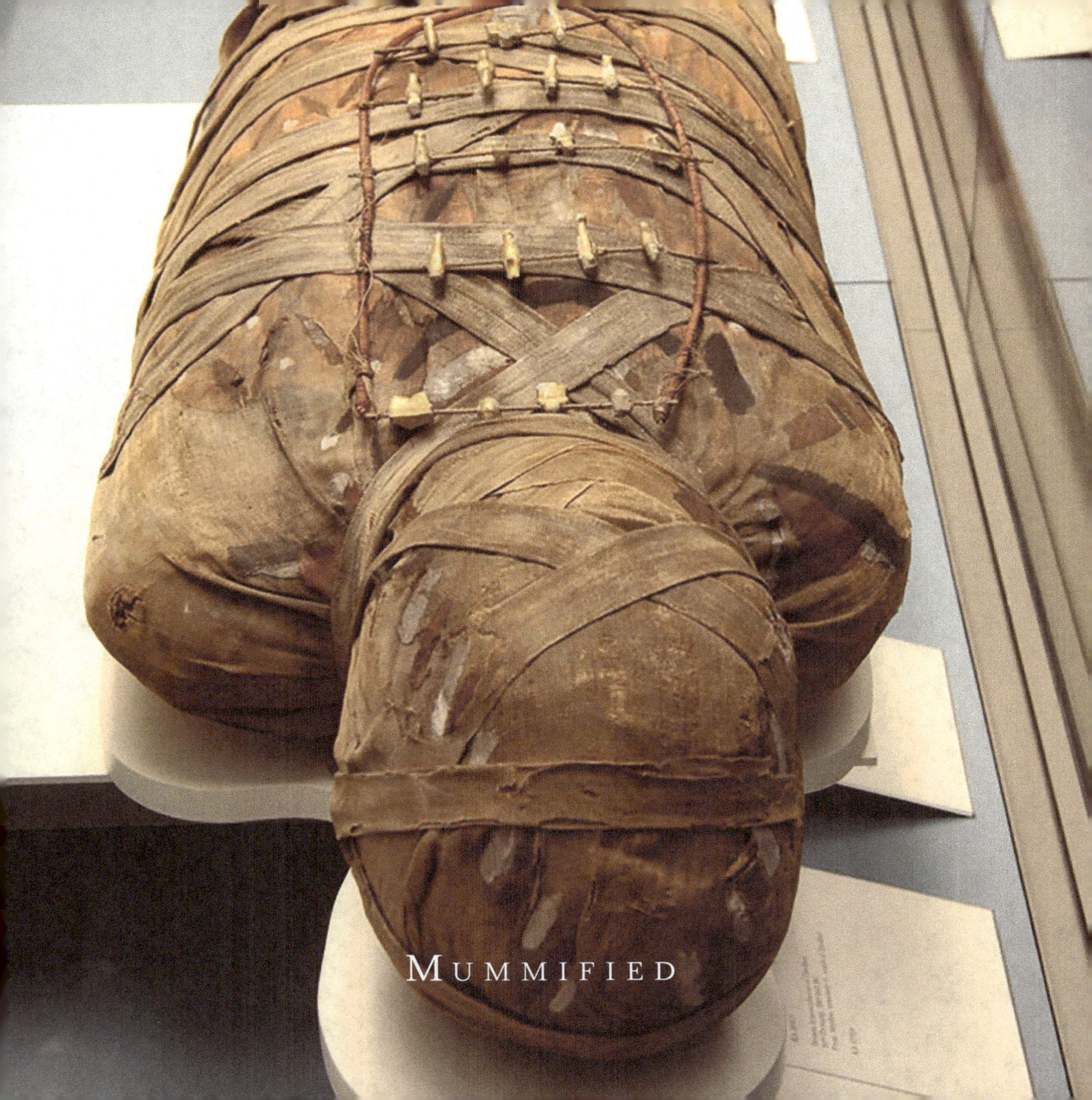

Mummified

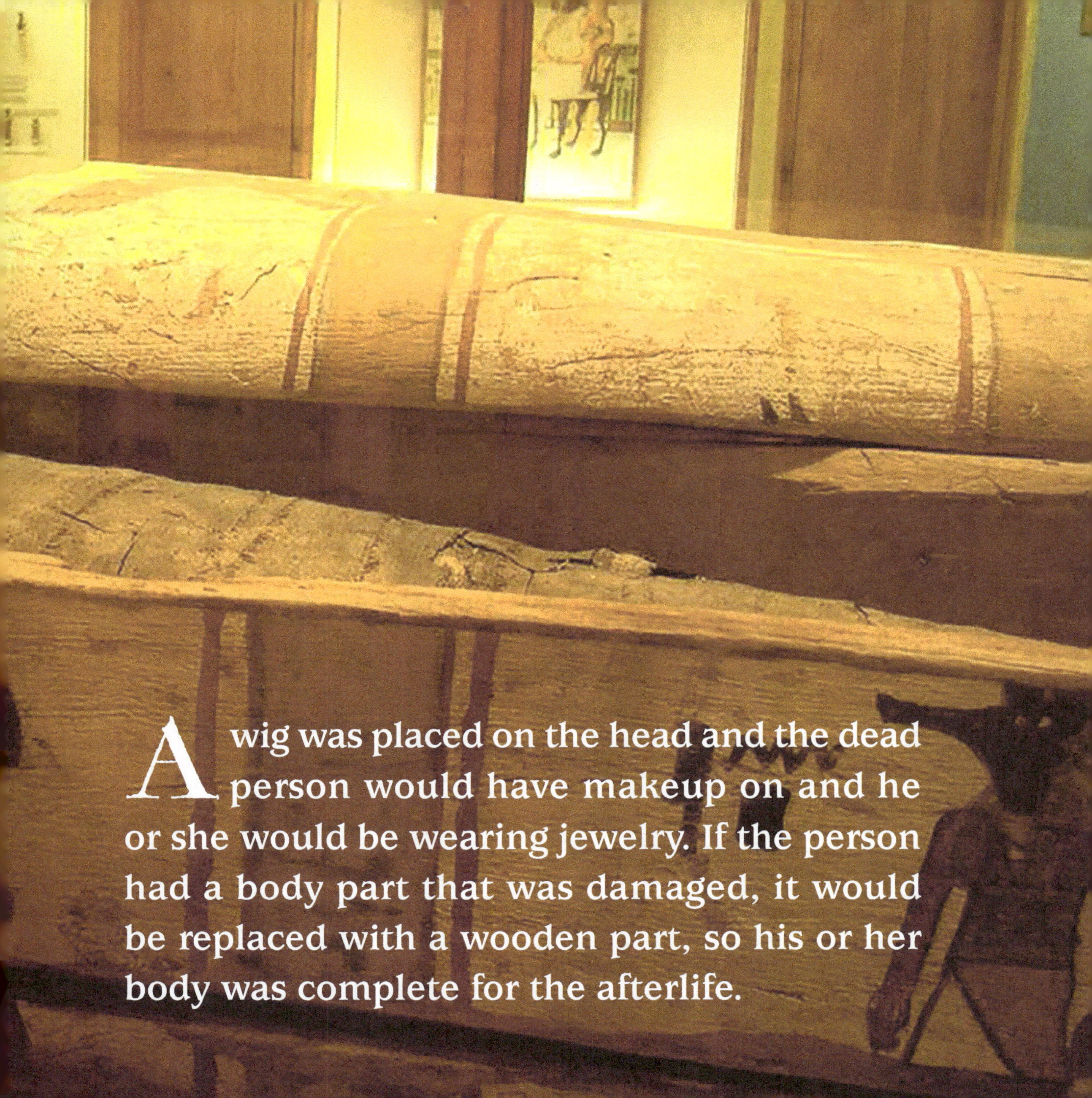

A wig was placed on the head and the dead person would have makeup on and he or she would be wearing jewelry. If the person had a body part that was damaged, it would be replaced with a wooden part, so his or her body was complete for the afterlife.

An amulet is a small object like a charm that is used for protection. Amulets, such as the sacred scarab amulet or the wedjat eye were placed on the body, sometimes in between the linen bandages.

S C A R A B   A M U L E T

The embalmers then carefully wrapped the body with the linen bandages. This part of the process may have taken up to two weeks. Religious rituals took place that were designed to help the person have a safe passage to his or her next life. A mask was placed on the body, and the body was placed inside the sarcophagus, which was a lifelike carved coffin.

Right before the sarcophagus was buried, there would be a ceremony called the "opening of the mouth." The temple priest would use special instruments to touch the face on the sarcophagus to restore the person's senses of sight, hearing, and taste for the afterlife.

The sarcophagus was then placed inside the tomb. It was surrounded by the person's possessions. Shabtis, which were small model

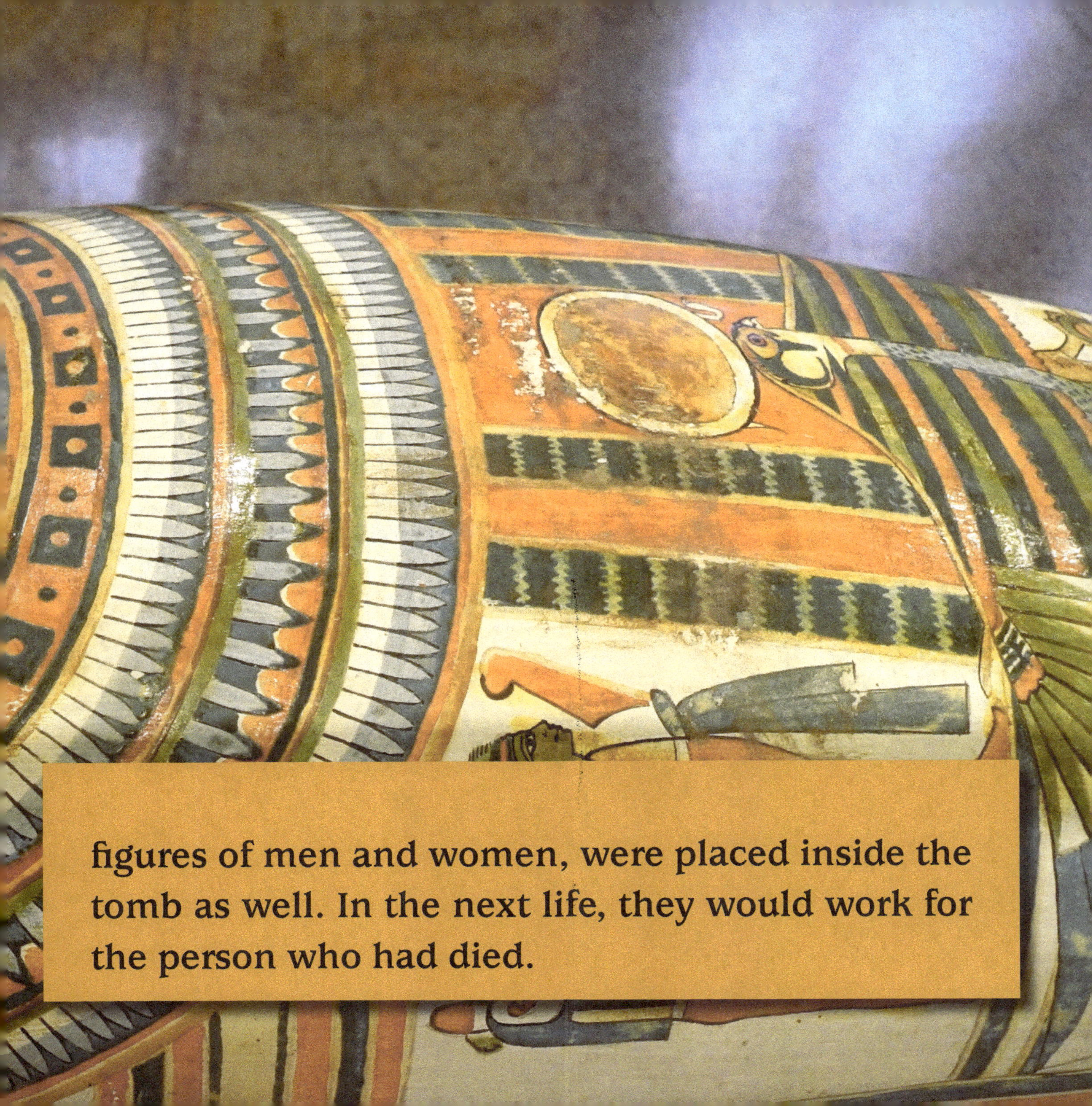

figures of men and women, were placed inside the tomb as well. In the next life, they would work for the person who had died.

THE CURSE OF THE MUMMY

There is a place in Egypt called the Valley of the Kings. Many tombs were located there, and many were robbed by treasure hunters. By the year 1914, many archaeologists thought that no other major discoveries would be found there. However, Howard Carter was one of the archaeologists who thought that the tomb of King Tut might still be found.

He looked and looked for over five years and found nothing. His investor, Lord Carnarvon said he would stop paying for his research if he didn't find something soon. Then, in 1922, after six years had passed since he began his search, Carter found a strange step underneath some huts. He found a stairway and a door to a tomb. He had finally found King Tutankhamun's tomb.

KING TUTANKHAMUN'S TOMB

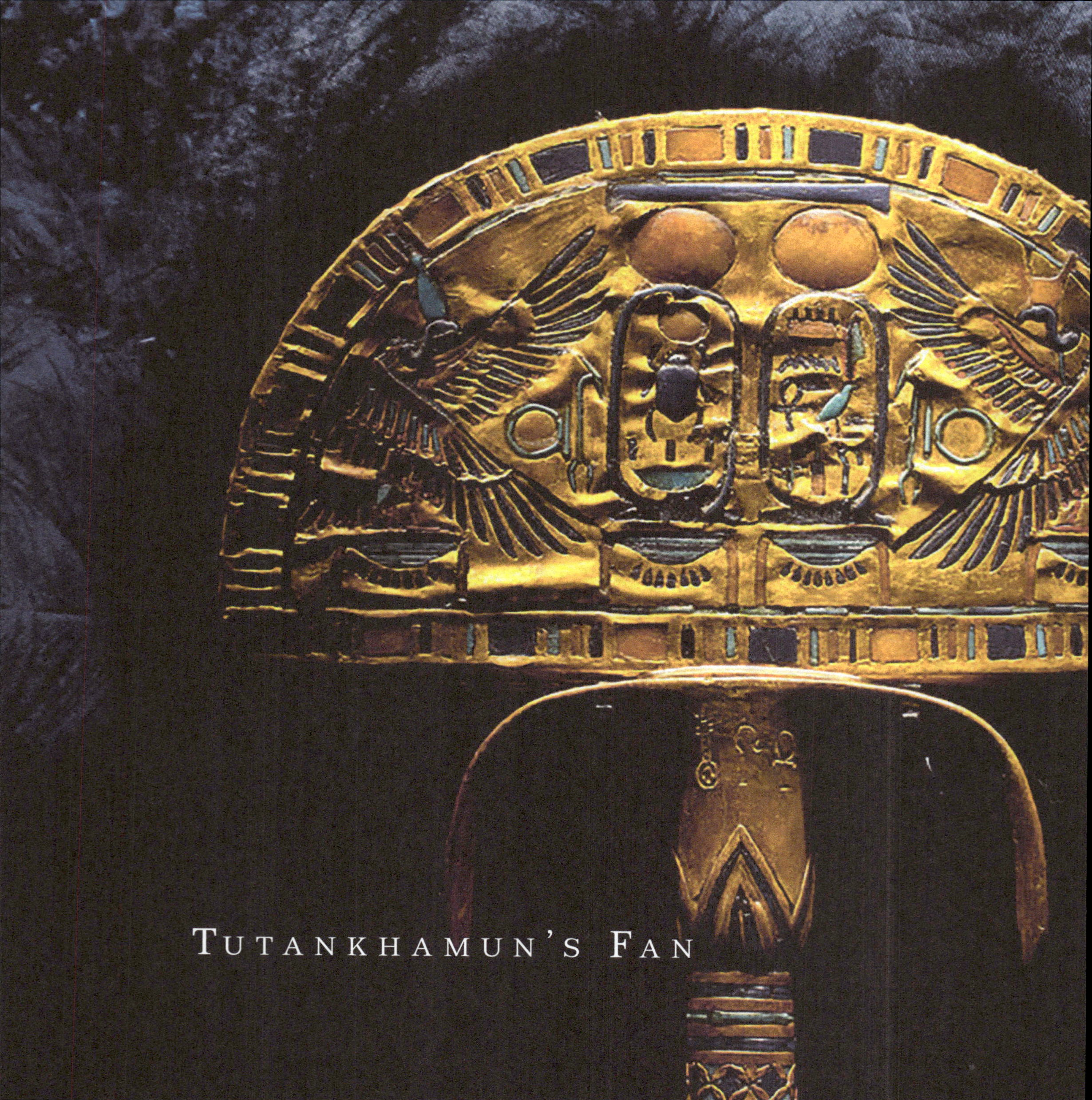

TUTANKHAMUN'S FAN

His discovery became one of the most important ever made. King Tut's mummy was there and amazing treasures of gold. There were over 5,000 of King Tut's possessions in the tomb. There were so many things it took a decade to catalog it all.

Many people thought that whoever was responsible for opening King Tut's tomb would be cursed. Within a yea,r Lord Carnarvon died from a mosquito bite. It was rumored that Carter's pet canary was devoured by a cobra on the exact day Carter had entered the tomb, but this wasn't true.

TUTANKHAMUN SCARAB

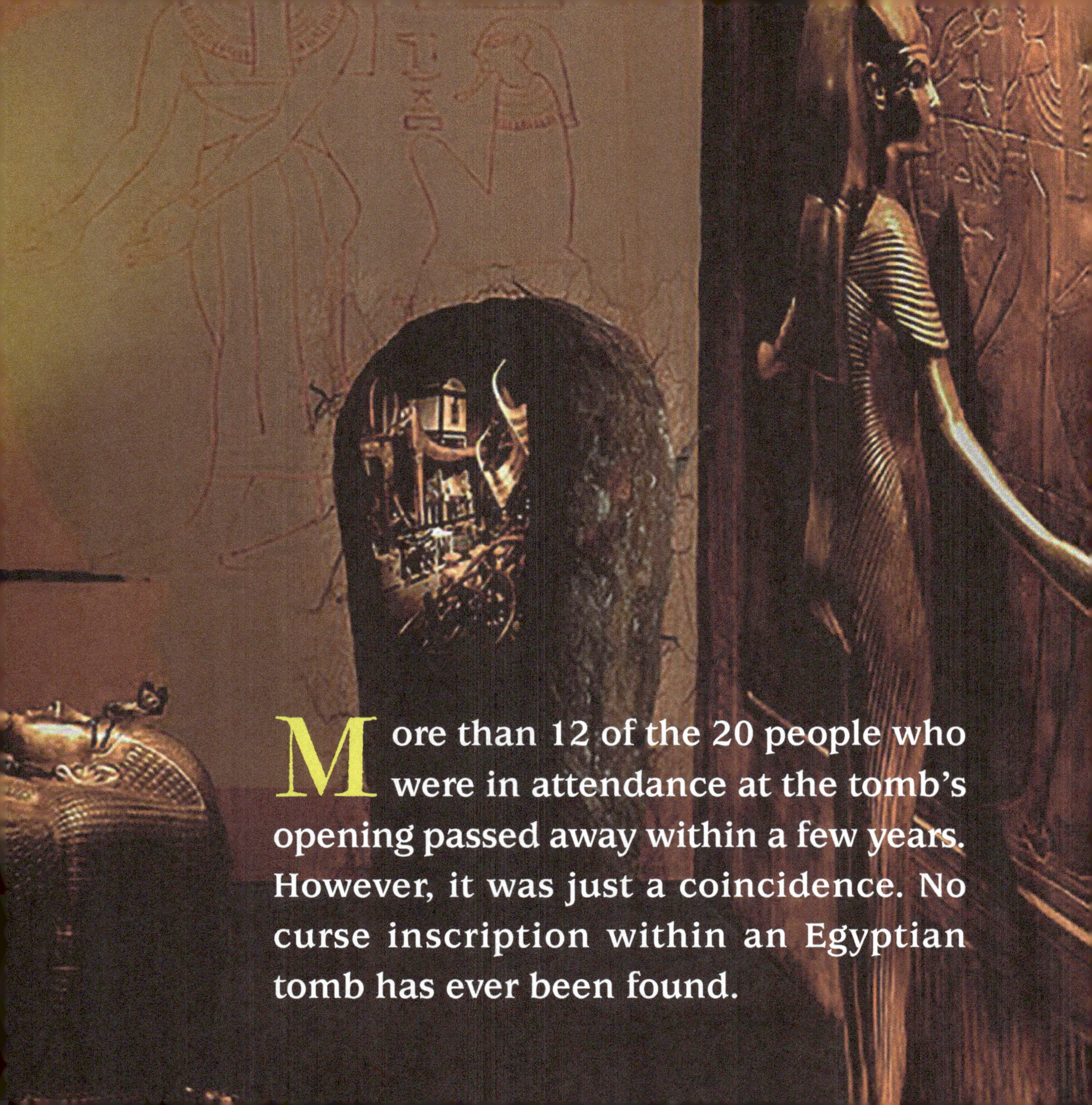

More than 12 of the 20 people who were in attendance at the tomb's opening passed away within a few years. However, it was just a coincidence. No curse inscription within an Egyptian tomb has ever been found.

FASCINATING FACTS ABOUT MUMMIES

Some Egyptian mummies have been preserved for eternity in museums, but this fate didn't happen for many of them. In the 1800s, it was thought that mummy powder could cure anything so it was used for magical potions and as medicine. Some mummies were destroyed by raiders looking for treasure. Others were thrown on fires to make fuel as if they were logs.

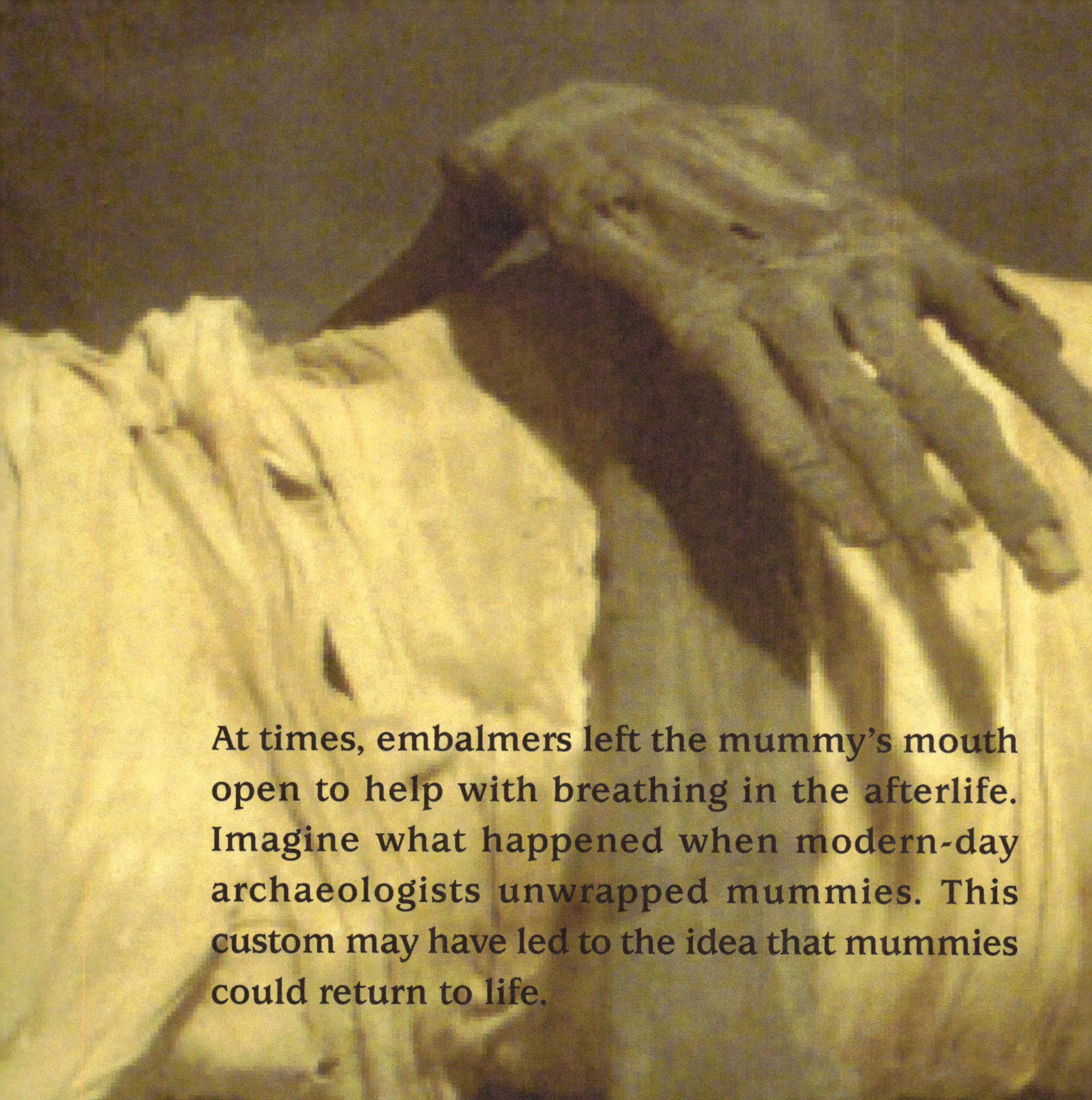

At times, embalmers left the mummy's mouth open to help with breathing in the afterlife. Imagine what happened when modern-day archaeologists unwrapped mummies. This custom may have led to the idea that mummies could return to life.

Archaeologists believe that over 70 million mummies were preserved in Egypt over their 3,000 years of civilization.

Q33
R32
R33
S32
R34

Some of Egypt's original Pharaohs can still be seen in mummy form. Ramesses II, one of the women Pharaohs called Hatshepsut, Tutankhamun called King Tut for short, and many others can be seen in museums today.

wesome! Now you know more about how and why the Egyptians created mummies and the mummy's curse. You can find more Ancient History books from Baby Professor by searching the website of your favorite book retailer.

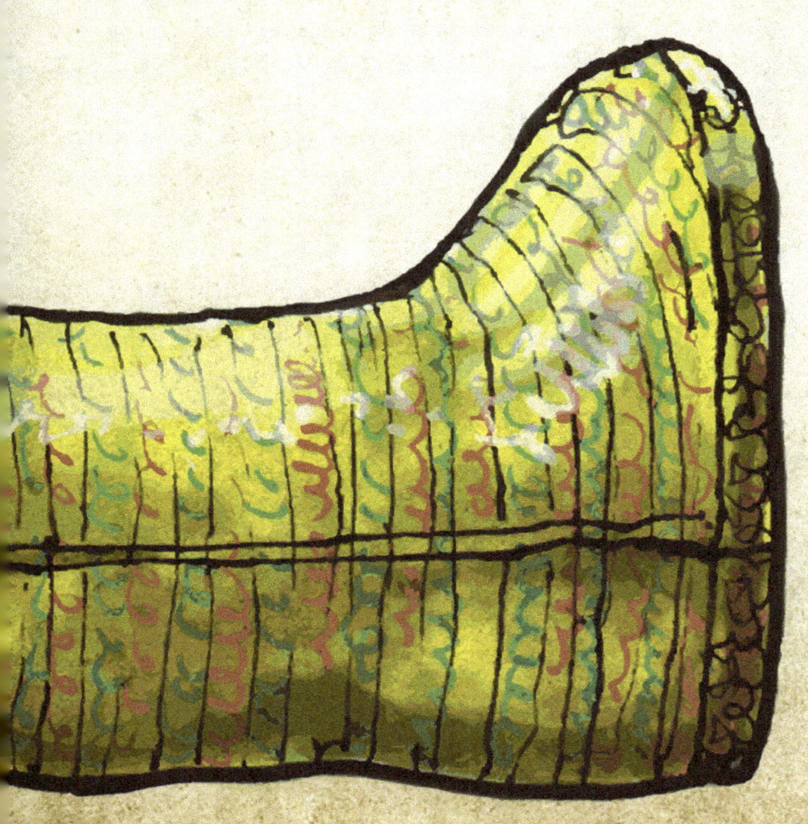

Visit
BABY PROFESSOR
EDUCATION KIDS
www.BabyProfessorBooks.com
to download Free Baby Professor eBooks and view
our catalog of new and exciting Children's Books